IPHONE SE

I0004275

A Complete User Guide For iPhone SE. Master Your Device, User Tips & Tricks, and Troubleshooting Hints.

Manuel Kay

Table of Content

Basic Functions.

Chapter Three

Calls and Contacts.

Introduction.

On April 2020 Apple unveiled the iPhone SE. The iPhone SE 2020 is coming as a follow up to the 2016 iPhone SE. According to Apple, the iPhone SE 2020 is the most affordable iPhone with its price at $399.

The 2020 iPhone SE share the same physical feature with the iPhone 8.It features a thick bottom and top bezels. The top bezel houses the 7-megapixel front camera and microphone, while the bottom bezel includes a Touch ID Home button for fingerprint. It also has a 4.7 inch Retina HD LCD display, with True Tone to match the ambient lighting in a room. It also features, Wide color, Dolby Vision, and HDR10.

The iPhone SE 2020 is available in Black, White and Red. It is built with a glass front and back, supports wireless charging and features 1P67 water and dust resistance.

The 2020 iPhone is the only device from the new generation iPhones that features a Touch ID over Face ID. It uses Haptic Touch for quick actions and contextual menus.

The device has a single lens 12 megapixel rear camera with an aperture of f/1.8. it also supports optical image stabilization, Portrait mode and portrait lightening. Although it doesn't have night mode, it has a Smart HDR, Wide Color support plus LED True Tone flash.

The iPhone SE camera can record 4K videos up to 60 frames per second with optical image stabilization, supports slow-mo video and time-lapse video. The front camera supports Portrait Mode and also uses the image signal processor and neural engine of A13 Bionic

The device is also equipped with a modern chip technology that features the same A13 Bionic chip like the iPhone 11. The A13 Bionic chip according to Apple is the fastest chip in a smart phone till date. The chip has a dedicated 8 core neural engine that can perform 5 trillion operations per second, two machine learning accelerators on the CPU, and a machine learning controller for better performance and efficiency.

The iPhone SE has a battery capacity of 13 hours when watching videos, 8 hours when streaming live videos, and 40 hours of audio listening. It has a fast charge feature and can charge to 50% in 3o minutes which using the 18w power adapter.

The device features a Wi-Fi and Bluetooth support.

Chapter One

How to insert your sim.

Note: Your **SIM** must be inserted before you can
use your mobile device.

- Fine the opener for the SIM holder inside

  the phone box.

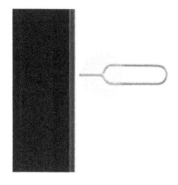

- Insert the opener into the small hole in the

  SIM holder area to pull out the **SIM tray**

- Carefully place your SIM into the SIM tray

  and insert the SIM tray back.

How to Activate your iPhone.
After inserting your SIM, you need to activate

your mobile phone before using it for the first

time. After you have restored your device to

factory setting, you also need to activate it once

again before use.

To Activate your device:

- Press the **Home key.**

- Select your **Language** of preference.

- Select the required **Country** or area.

- If your **SIM i**s locked, enter your PIN and

  tap OK. The default **SIM PIN IS 0000.**

- **Note:** If you enter wrong PIN three time your SIM will be blocked and would require PUK to be unblock. To obtain your SIM PUK, you can contact the customer care service of your network provider. If you enter the wrong PUK ten times, your SIM will be blocked permanently.
- After entering your PIN, follow the on-screen instructions to transfer content from your former iOS device if you had one, or Tap **Set Up Manually to proceed.**
- On the next page, a list of available **Wi-Fi networks** will be displayed, select the required **Wi-Fi network and enter the password carefully**, then tap Join.

- **Note:** If there is no Wi-Fi network available, you can use your mobile network.

- After joining a Wi-Fi network, you will be ushered to the **Data and Privacy page, tap on Continue.**

- On the next page, you can follow the on-screen instructions to turn on **Touch ID** or tap on **Set Up Touch ID Later.** How to set up touch ID will be treated later in page …..

- You will get a prompt asking if you are sure you don't want to use **Touch ID, tap on Don't Use.**

- On the next page, you will be required to create a **password to protect your data and unlock your phone.** Tap on **Passcode Options.**

- Follow the on-screen instructions to turn on use of **Phone lock Code, or** tap on Don't Use Passcode.

- If you selected **Don't use passcode,** you will get a prompt on the screen of your device. Again, tap **Don't use passcode**. How to set up passcode will be treated in page …..

- On the **Apps & Data page**, tap on **Don't transfer Apps & Data,** then follow the on-screen instructions to finish activation.

How to restore backed data from iCloud.
If you previously used an iOS device and have

some data backed up on the cloud. You can restore

the backed up data to your new iPhone device. By

restoring this data, you are moving all the content

and settings from your old device to your new

device.

To restore data from iCloud:

- During your set up process, when you get to

  this page

- Select **Restore from iCloud Backup**

- On the next page, you will be required to

  enter your **Apple ID email and password.**

  Enter them correctly and proceed.

- **Agree to the terms and conditions**

- On the next page you will see dates of

  backups on the screen of your device. Tap

on the most recent backup date and follow the on-screen instructions.

- It will take a moment for your device to restore backup completely.

How to transfer content from your Android mobile device to your iPhone device.

You can transfer content from your android device to you iPhone device when it is activated.

To transfer content from android to iPhone:

- When this screen is displayed on your device during set up, your device is ready to transfer content from an android mobile device.

- Select **Move Data from Android.**

- To be able to transfer data from your **Android to your iOS device**, you need to download an app on your android device.

The app is **'Move to iOS'.** Download it and
have it installed.

- When the app is installed on your android
  device, come back to your iPhone and tap on
  Continue.
- Carefully follow the instructions on the
  screen of your device to transfer content
  from your android to iOS.

How to Charge Your Phone Battery.

Endeavor to charge your device regularly to ensure

that it is always ready to use.

- Connect the charger to charging port of your

  phone.

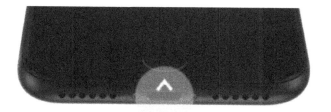

- One the phone is charging, the battery icon

  at the top right hand side of your device will

  indicate by turning to green.

- When your device is fully charged, remove the charger from the charging port and unplug the adapter from power source.

How to activate Apple ID on your mobile device. Apple ID gives you access to several functions on your mobile device. With Apple ID you can maximize the usage of your device. When you have an apple ID, functions like App Store, iCloud, Apple Music, etc. are opened to you.

To activate your Apple ID.

- Locate and tap on **Settings** on the **Home Screen** of your device.

- Tap on **Sign In to your iPhone**

- If you have an Apple ID, enter the **email address** associated with it in the email column and tap **Next** and the top right side of your device.

- Enter your **password and tap on Next again.**

- If you don't have or forgot your Apple ID, tap on **'Don't have an Apple ID or Forgot It'**

- Carefully follow the instructions on the screen of your device to create an **Apple ID.**

- Once you have completed creating your Apple ID, tap on the **home button to return to the home screen.**

How to choose a network.
You can set your mobile device to find a network automatically or manually. When you select a network manually, the network connection will be lost once you are out of range.

To select a network.

- Locate the **Settings** icon on your home screen and tap on it.

- Locate and tap on **Mobile Data** on the settings page.

- Locate and tap on **Network Selection** on the Mobile Data page.

- Toggle the indictor next to automatic to turn Off automatic network selection.

- Tap on any option of your choice between **Network 1 and Network 2** below automatic.

- Tap on the **home button to return to home screen.**

How to turn mobile data On/Off.
Turning off your mobile data helps you limit data

usage on your device. When your mobile data is

turned off, you cannot access the internet.

To turn On/Off your mobile data.

- Locate the **Settings** icon on your home

  screen and tap on it.

- Locate and tap on **Mobile Data** on the

  settings page.

- Toggle the indicator next to mobile data

  On/Off.

- You can go further and turn **On/Off** the applications you don't want to use your mobile data or turn them on.

- Tap on the home button to return to home screen.

How to divert calls to your voicemail.

In order to receive voice messages when you don't answer a call, you have to divert your calls to your voicemail.

- Locate the **Phone icon** and tap on it

- Locate the **keypad icon** and tap on it.

- Enter these digits ****21*+61411000321#**

  and dial.

- Enter the required number of seconds before

  the call is diverted and dial. Note: the

  number must be divisible by 5, e.g. 25.

  digits **21*+61411000321*25#

- A list of options will appear on the screen of your device, tap dismiss.

- Tap the home key to return to the home screen of your device.

How to turn On do not disturb.

If you don't want to be disturbed, you can restrict call, messages, or notifications from entering your phone by activating the do not disturb feature for a specific period of time. In activating do not disturb, you can choose for your phone to ring when certain contacts call you.

To activate do not disturb:

- Locate the **Settings Icon** on your home screen and tap on it.

- Scroll down on the setting page and tap on **Do Not Disturb.**

- Activate **Do Not Disturb** turn the indicator next to it On.

- Turn on the indicator next to **'Scheduled'** under do not disturb and follow the instructions to select the timeframe you want your device to be on do not disturb.

- If you want to set your mobile phone to permanent **Do Not Disturb,** tap on **Always.**

- If you want your device to be on **DO NOT DISTURB** only when your iPhone is locked, tap on **While iPhone is Locked**

- To permit certain calls to come in when your phone is on **Do Not Disturb,** tap on **Allow Calls From.**

- Tap the required option you want to get calls from when your do not disturb is on.

- Tap on the **Back menu** at the top left corner of your device screen.

- Tap on the indicator next to **'Repeated Calls'** to turn the function **On/Off**

- Tap on **'Activate'**

- Tap on the required setting.

- Go back to the **Do Not Disturb page** and tap on **'Auto-Reply To'**

- Tap on the required setting to select the group of contact that should automatically be notified that your Do Not Disturb While Driving is turned On.

- Go back to the **Do Not Disturb page** and tap on **Auto-Reply.**

- Follow the on-screen instructions to edit the automatic message that your device will send when you do not disturb while driving is on.

- Tap the home key to return to the home screen of your device.

How to turn flight mode On/Off.
Turning on flight mode prevents your device from causing interference with sensitive equipment in a plane or hospital. When your device is on flight mode, you can not make calls or send messages.

To activate flight mode:

- **Swipe up** from the bottom end of your device to bring out some quick settings.

- The flight mode is represent by an **airplane icon.**

- Tap on the icon to turn the function **On/Off.**

- Tap the home key to return to the home screen of your device.

How to turn Wi-Fi On/Off.
Wi-fi network serves as an alternative to mobile network. When you device is connected to a Wi-Fi it doesn't use your mobile data to surf the internet.

To turn Wi-Fi On/Off:

- Locate the **Settings icon** on your home screen and tap on it.

- Tap on **Wi-Fi** on the list of functions.

- Toggle the indicator next to the function to turn it **On/Off.**

- Tap the home key to return to the home screen of your device.

How to end running Applications.

When your iPhone device returns to home screen, sometimes, some applications are still running on the background. Most time these applications running on the background causes your battery to drain quickly.

To end running applications:

- Tap on the **home key twice**, this action will file out all recently used and running applications.

- **Swipe up** on each application page to end it.

- Tap the home key to return to the home screen of your device.

How to Turn Screen Lock On/Off.

When the screen lock of your device is turned on, it prevents you from activating your device by mistake.

To activate Screen Lock:

- Tap the **Power button** once to expose the screen light.

- Tap on the home key to **Unlock** your device.

- Locate the settings icon on your home screen and tap on it.

- Locate and tap on **Display & Brightness.**

- Tap on **Auto-lock**

- Choose the required time you would like your phone to be On before auto-locking.

- Tap the home key to return to the home screen of your device.

How to choose setting for the control center.

The control center is that shortcut panel that appears when you swipe up from the bottom of your device. You can choose the settings to appear on this panel.

To choose the settings:

- Locate the **Settings icon** on your home screen and tap on it.

- Tap on **Control Center** on the settings page.

- Activate or deactivate by toggling the indicator next to **Access Within Apps.**

- When the function is turned on, the **Control Center** can be used on the home screen and also while using other applications.

- To customize control center, tap on

  'Customize Controls'.

- Tap on the **delete icon** on red to remove a

  function from the control center. Tap the

  green + icon beside the apps to add them to

  the control center.

- Tap on the move icon next to the added apps to move them to the location of our choice in the control center.

- Tap the home key to return to the home screen of your device.

How to use the control center.
The control center helps you to quickly access

function on your iPhone device.

To use the control center:

- Swipe up from the bottom end of your

  device.

- The control center will be displayed. Tap on

  any icon of your choice to activate the

  functions.

- Tap the home key to return to the home

  screen of your device.

How to activate and choose Siri Settings.

Siri is the voice assistance on your phone. With Siri you can control many functions on your device with your voice. You can dial numbers, dictate messages and search the internet without typing on your phone.

To activate Siri:

- Locate the **Settings icon** on your home screen and tap on it.
- Tap on **Siri & Search** on the settings page.
- Select **Press Home for Siri** and toggle the indicator next to it to turn it **On.**

- Tap on **Enable Siri** on the pop up that will appear on your screen.

- Activate **Listen for Hey Siri** on. Once this function is turned on, you need to follow the on-screen instructions to set up Siri to recognize your voice.

- On the **Siri and Search page**, tap on **Language.**

- Select your preferred **Language for Siri.**

- Return to the **Siri and Search page** and tap on **Siri Voice.**

- On the Siri Voice page, choose **Siri's accent and Gender.**

- Return to the Siri & Search page, tap on **Voice Feedback.**

- Select **Always On,** This means that Siri will provide feedback even when your ring switch is set to silent.

- **Return to Siri & Search page.**

- Tap the home key to return to the home screen of your device.

Chapter Two

Basic Functions.

How to turn On/Off silent mode.

When you turn your iPhone device to silent mode,
all phone sounds re turned off.

To turn silent mode On/Off.

- **Flip the silent mode button right or left to
  activate silent mode.**

How to turn Vibration On/Off.

When your iPhone device is turned to vibration, it vibrates when there is an incoming call.

To turn vibration On/Off:

- Tap on **Settings** on the **Home screen** of your device.

- On the **Settings page,** tap on **Sounds & Haptics.**

- On the Sounds & Haptics page, toggle the indicator next to **Vibrate OnRing** to turn it On/Off. Do the same to **Vibrate on Silent.**

- Tap the home key to return to the home screen of your device.

How to change Screen Brightness.
You can manage the screen brightness of your device to fit your surroundings.

To manage screen brightness:

- Tap on **Settings** on the Home screen of your device.

- On the Settings page, tap on **Display & Brightness.**

- On the display and brightness page, drag the indicator below Brightness right or left to increase or reduce the brightness of your screen.

- Return to Settings page.

- Tap on **Accessibility.**

- On Accessibility page, tap on **Display & Text Size.**

- Scroll down on Display and Text page and tap on turn **Auto-Brightness On/Off.**
- Tap the home key to return to the home screen of your device.

How to turn use of SIM PIN On/Off.

Your PIN protects your SIM card from unauthorized use if your device get lost or stolen. If the use of PIN is turn on, once your mobile device is powered, you will be required to enter your PIN.

To activate or deactivate this function:

- Tap on **Settings** on the Home screen of your device.

- Scroll down on the settings page and tap on **Mobile Data.**

- On the mobile data page, scroll down and tap on **SIM PIN**

- Toggle the indicator next to **SIM PIN.** To turn it **On/Off.**

- On the next page, enter your **PIN** and tap on Done at the top right side of your device screen. The default PIN is **0000.**

- Note:*If you enter wrong PIN three times your SIM will be blocked and would require PUK to be unblock. To obtain your SIM PUK, you can contact the customer care service of your network provider. If you enter the wrong PUK ten times, your SIMwill be blocked permanently.*

- To change PIN

- Return to SIM PIN page, and tap on **Change PIN.**

- Enter your current PIN and tap on Done.

- On the next page, enter your new 4-digit pin and tap **Done.**

- Confirm new pin by entering it again after which you tap on Done.

- Tap the home key to return to the home screen of your device.

How to back up your phone memory to iCloud.
Backing up your phone memory to iCloud ensures that no data is lost when you update your iPhone software, or when your device goes missing or lost. To be able to back up your device memory, you need to have an **Apple ID and a Wi-Fi connection.**

To back up:

- Tap on **Settings** on the Home screen of your device.

- Tap on your **Apple ID.**

- On your Apple ID page scroll down and tap on **iCloud.**

- On iCloud page, scroll **down and tap on iCloud Backup.**

- **Turn ON iCloud Backup.**

- A prompt will appear on your screen asking to **'Start iCloud Backup'** tap **OK.** Your phone memory will automatically get backed up when your phone is charging, and you are connected to a Wi-Fi network.

- Tap **Back Up now** and wait while the phone memory is backed up.

- Tap the home key to return to the home screen of your device.

How to restore your phone to factory settings.
When your iPhone device gets slow or doesn't

function as it should, it may require that you

restore it to the factory default settings. When your

iPhone is restored to factory settings, all settings

and configurations you've made to the phone is

deleted.

To Restore to factory settings:

- Tap on **Settings** on the Home screen of your

  device.

- Locate and tap on **General** on the settings

  page.

- Scroll down and tap on Reset.

- Tap on **Reset All Settings.** A prompt will appear asking that you confirm your request, tap on **Reset All Setting.** Wait a moment while your phone restores to factory settings. Carefully follow the instructions on the screen of your device to prepare for use.

- **Note: *When you choose reset all settings, your contacts, audio files, video clips and appointments will not be deleted.***

- To erase all content and settings, go back to the Reset page and tap **'Erase All Content and Settings.'**

- A prompt will pop up asking if you want to update your iCloud backup before erasing. If you have not backed up your device content to iCloud choose **Back Up then Reset.** If you have backed up your device content, then choose **Erase Now.**

- If you choose Erase Now, a pop-up will appear reminding you that all media and data will be deleted also all settings will be reset. Tap on **Erase iPhone.**

- Another prompt will appear asking if you are sure, tap on **Erase iPhone** again.

- You will be requested to enter your **Apple ID password.** After you have entered your **Apple ID password,** wait a moment while your device restores to factory settings.

How to set up notifications.
You can set your iPhone to display notifications about new messages, appointments, missed calls, etc. in the status bar at the top of your device screen.

To manage notifications:

- Tap on **Settings** on the Home screen of your device.

- On the settings page, tap on **Notifications.**

- On the notification page tap on **Show Preview.**

- Tap on **Always** to select notification preview on locked screen.

- To view notification preview only when your iPhone is unlocked, tap on **When Unlocked.**

- To turn off notification preview, tap on **Never.**

- If you selected **Always or When Unlocked**, return to the notifications page and tap on **App store.**

- Tap on **Allow notification** on App Store page. Do the same on all application you'd like to receive notifications from.

- Tap the home key to return to the home screen of your device.

How to Set Up and Use Touch ID.

You can easily set up your iPhone to use your fingerprint as phone lock code, or to authorize purchases on your device. To use Touch ID, you need to take the following steps.

- Tap on **Settings** on the Home screen of your device.

- Locate and tap on **Touch ID & Passcode.**

- On Touch ID & Passcode page, tap on **Add a Fingerprint**. Follow the on-screen instructions to add your finger print.

- Tap on **Continue** after adding your fingerprint

- Toggle On the indicator next to **'iPhone Unlock, iTunes & App Store, Apple Pay, and Password Autofill.'** Turning On these functions will authorize your iPhone to use your fingerprint when the need arises on those functions.

- Tap the home key to return to the home screen of your device.

How to turn GPS On/Off.

Your iPhone can determine your geographical location using the GPS. The information about your location can be used by some application on your device for navigation, weather forecast, etc.

To turn GPS On/Off:

- Tap on **Settings** on the Home screen of your device.

- Scroll down on the settings page and tap on **Privacy.**

- Tap on **Location Services** on privacy page.

- Toggle the indicator next to location service to turn it **On/Off**

- Scroll down again and enable some apps to share your location, example **Camera.**

- Tap on **'While Using the App.'**

- Tap the home key to return to the home screen of your device.

How to set up and use Dark Mode.

With the introduction of dark theme, you can use your iPhone in dark surrounding with inconveniencing others. You can also create a schedule for your device to move in and out of dark mode at certain times.

To activate Dark Mode:

- Tap on **Settings** on the Home screen of your device.

- Tap on **Display and Brightness.**

- Tap on **Dark.**

- Tap on the indicator next to **Automatic** to turn the function **On/Off**

- Once you have turned On Dark Mode, tap on **Options** under it and follow the on-scree instructions to select the required period of time for Dark Mode.

- Tap the home key to return to the home screen of your device.

How to choose Night Shift Settings.

You can set your iPhone to adjust the screen colors depending on the changing daylight.

To choose Night Shift Settings:

- Tap on **Settings** on the Home screen of your device.

- Tap on **Display and Brightness.**

- Scroll to the bottom of the page and tap on **Night Shift**

- On Night Shift page, tap on **Scheduled** and turn it On. Follow the instructions on the screen to select the required period of time for Night Shift.

- Tap on the indicator next to **'Manually Enable Until Tomorrow'** to turn on Night Shift immediately.

- Scroll down, tap and drag the indicator below **'COLOR TEMPERATURE'** either right or light to select the required color temperature.

- Tap the home key to return to the home screen of your device.

Chapter Three

Calls and Contacts.

How to call a phone number.
The major essence of having a phone is to be able

to make calls.

To make call:

- Tap on the phone icon on your home screen.

- Tap on the **Keypad** shortcut.

- Enter the required phone number and tap the

call icon.

How to turn call waiting On/Off

The call waiting function when turned on allows you to answer a new call without ending an ongoing call.

This function can be turned On/Off by:

- Tap on **Settings** on the Home screen of your device.
- On settings page, scroll down and tap on **Phone.**
- Tap on **Call Waiting** on the Phone page.

- Toggle the indicator beside **Call Waiting to turn it On/Off.**

- Tap on the home button to return to the home screen.

How to save a voicemail number.
You can save a voicemail number which will make it easier for you to call and listen to your voice messages.

To save a voicemail number:

- Once you insert your SIM into your phone, the voice mail number is saved automatically.

How to cancel all call divert

If at any point you no longer wish to divert calls coming to your phone, you need to cancel all call divert.

To cancel all diverts:

- Tap on the **Phone icon** on the home screen of your device.

- Tap on the **keypad icon.**

- Type **##002#** and tap on the call icon.

- A display with all the divert options will appear on your screen, tap on **Dismiss.**
- Tap on the home button to return to the home screen.

How to turn Call announcement On/Off.
You can set your iPhone to announce the contact that's calling you when a call comes through your device. If the number is not saved on your address book, your device will call out the digits.

To set call announcement:

- Tap on **Settings** on the Home screen of your device.

- On settings page, scroll down and tap on **Phone.**

- Tap on **Announce Calls** on the Phone page

- On the next page, select **Always.**

- If you don't want your device to announce callers ID, select **Never.**

- Select **Headphones & Car** to turn on the function when your iPhone device is connected to a headset or your car.

- Tap on **Headphones Only** to turn on the function when your device is connected to a headset.

- Tap on the home button to return to the home screen.

How to Import Contacts from your SIM to your mobile Phone.

You can import your SIM contacts to your iPhone so that your contact remains intact even if you lose your SIM.

To import contacts to your iPhone:

- Tap on **Settings** on the Home screen of your device.

- Tap on **Contacts** on thee settings page.

- Scroll down and tap on **Import SIM Contacts.**

- Tap on the home button to return to the home screen.

How to copy contacts from social network sites and email accounts.

You can copy the contacts from your email accounts and social network sites to the address book of your phone. Before you can copy contacts from these places, your device needs to be connected to the internet.

To copy contacts:

- Tap on **Settings** on the Home screen of your device.

- Tap on **Passwords & Accounts** on the settings page.

- Tap on **Gmail** on the passwords & Accounts page.

- Turn on the indicator next to Contact on the Gmail page.

- Tap on the home button to return to the home screen.

How to block a phone number.

If you don't want to receive voice calls or messages from number(s), you can block them. When a blocked number calls you, your number will give them a busy signal.

To block a number.

- Tap on the **Phone** icon on the home screen of your device.

- Tap on **Recent.**

- Tap on the **information icon** next to the number you wish to block.

- Scroll down and tap on **Block this Caller**. A prompt will appear notifying you that you will not receive calls and messages from the number when blocked.

- Confirm by tapping on **Block Contact.**

- Tap on the home button to return to the home screen.

How to merge Identical contacts.

If you have two identical numbers on your phone's address book, you can merge them to appear only once.

To merge identical contacts.

- Tap on **Contacts** on the home screen of your device.

- Tap on the required **Contact.**

- Tap on **Edit** at the top right corner of your device.

- Scroll down and tap on **Link Contacts.**

- Tap on the second contact you want linked.

- Tap on **Link** at the top right corner of your device.

- Tap on the home button to return to the home screen.

Chapter Four

Messages and Email.

How to set up your mobile phone for iMessaging.

You can send iMessage to other contacts on your address book that has iPhone. Beware that before you can send iMessage you need to activate your Apple ID.

To set up your Phone for iMessaging:

- Tap on **Settings** on the Home screen of your device.

- Scroll down an tap on **Messages** on settings page.

- Toggle the indicator to turn iMeesage function On.

- Scroll down on the same page and turn on **'Send as SMS,'** This means your iMessge will be sent as SMS if the service is not available.

- Tap on the home button to return to the home screen.

How to set up your phone for MMS.

MMS (Multi Media Message) is a message that contain pictures and media files. Once you insert your SIM to your phone, you can send MMS message, but if that's not the case, then you can set up your device to send MMS manually.

To set up phone for MMS:

- Tap on **Settings** on the Home screen of your device.

- Scroll down an tap on **Messages** on settings page.

- Scroll down the list of options and activate **MMS Messaging.**

- Tap on the home button to return to the home screen.

How to set up your iPhone for POP3 email.

You can set up your mobile phone to send and receive emails from your email accounts. With the POP3, your emails are retrieved and stored on your mobile device and deleted from the server, this makes it impossible to access your email from different devices. Before you set up your device for POP3 emails, it must be connected to the internet.

To set up your device for POP3:

- Tap on **Settings** on the Home screen of your device.

- Tap on **Passwords & Accounts.**

- Tap on **Add Account.**

- Scroll down the list of email options and tap on **Others** if your email provider is not listed.

- Tap on **Add Mail Account.**

- Carefully key in the required details and tap on **Next** at the top right corner of your device and tap on **Next**

- If the above screen is displayed, then your email account has been recognized and set up automatically. Carefully follow the instructions on the screen of your device to enter more information and finish setting up your mobile phone.

- Tap on **POP** of the **New Account page.**

- Scroll down and tap on **Host name.** Enter the name of your email provider's incoming serve.

- Tap on **Username** and enter the username of your email account.

- Tap on **Host Name** under outgoing mail servers and enter the same host name as provided before.

- Tap on Save at the top right corner of your device. Your email account has been set up.

- Tap on the home button to return to the home screen.

How to set up your device for IMAP email

You can set up your mobile phone to send and receive emails from your email accounts. With the IMAP, your emails are retrieved and stored on your mobile device and kept on the server, this makes it possible to access your email from different devices. Before you set up your device for IMAP emails, it must be connected to the internet.

To set up your device for IMAP email:

- Tap on **Settings** on the Home screen of your device.

- Tap on **Passwords & Accounts.**

- Tap on **Add Account.**

- Scroll down the list of email options and tap on Others if your email provider is not listed.

- Tap on **Add Mail Account.**

- Carefully key in the required details and tap on Next at the top right corner of your device and tap on Next.

- Tap on **IMAP** on the next page.

- Scroll down and tap on **Host name.** Enter
  the name of your email provider's incoming
  serve.

- Tap on **Username** and enter the username of
  your email account.

- Tap on **Host Name** under outgoing mail
  servers and enter the same host name as
  provided before.

- Tap on **Save** at the top right corner of your device. Your email account has been set up.

- Tap on the home button to return to the home screen.

How to set up your mobile phone for Exchange email.

You can set up your iPhone device to send and receive emails from **Exchanger email account.** Your device needs to be connected to the internet to execute this function.

To set up your device for Exchanger email:

- Tap on **Settings** on the Home screen of your device.

- Tap on **Passwords & Accounts.**

- Tap on **Add Account.**

- Tap on email and enter the email address.

- Tap on **Description** and enter the required name. Tap on **Next** to move to the next page.

- A prompt will appear on the screen of your device. Tap on **Sign In.**

- Tap on **Sign In**

- Toggle the indicators next to the required data types to turn synchronization of each data On/Off.

- Tap on **Save** afterwards. Your email has been set up.

- Tap on the home button to return to the home screen.

How to set a default email account.
If you have more than one email account set up on your mobile device you can select a default email account. This enables all your outgoing emails to go through one email account unless you are prompted to select a different account before sending.

To set up a default email account:

- Tap on **Settings** on the Home screen of your device.

- Tap on **Mail** on the next page.

- Scroll down and select **Default Account.**

- Tap on any option between. **'Groupwm or Gmail'** to select either one as a default account.

- Tap on the home button to return to the home screen.

Chapter Five

Applications and Data Management.

How to install apps from App Store.
Once you've set up your iPhone for internet and Apple ID created, you can download apps to your device from the app store.

To download Apps:

- Tap on the **App Store** app on the home screen of your device.

- Tap on the **Search** icon at the bottom right corner of the App Store page.

- Type the name of the Application you wish to download on the search bar.

- A list of application will appear as your key in the name of your desired application. Once you see the App, click on it.

- Tap on **GET** at the apps page and follow the instructions on the screen of the device to install the app

- Tap on the home button to return to the home screen.

How to uninstall apps.

You can uninstall apps that you don't have any need for to free up space on your device.

To uninstall apps:

- **Force press** on the app.

- An options menu will appear, tap on **Delete App**. This will delete the App and its settings from the phone memory.

- A prompt will appear asking you to confirm your request, tap on **Delete.**

- Tap on the home button to return to the home screen.

How to transfer files between your iPhone and windows PC.

You can transfer files likes audio and video files, pictures and documents between your phone and your computer. Depending on the Windows OS you are running on, the instructions may differ.

Let's get started.

- Ensure that you have **installed iTunes** on your computer.

- Connect the USB cable to your phone and computer.

- On your PC, click on **iTunes.** Ensure that you have added the needed files to your iTunes.

- On the iTunes page, click on **Files** at the upper left corner of your device.

- On the drop down menu that appears, click on **Add File to Library.**

- Go to the folder where the required file is in your computer and follow the on-screen instructions to have it added to your iTunes.

- If your iTunes is set to automatic transfer, it will start transferring your files immediately.

- To manually transfer the files, click on the iPhone icon on your iTunes page.

- Click on the required category which could be Music, Video, etc. and follow the on-screen instructions to select the required

settings.

- Click on **Apply** at the end of your PC

  screen.

- Open the **File Manager** on your PC.

- Navigate to the required folder on your

  iPhone file system.

- Select the required files and move/copy

  them to the required location.

How to synchronize contents of your iPhone using iCloud.

When you synchronize the content of your iPhone

using the iCloud, it enables you to access the

content anywhere with different devices. You can

also restore them to a new iPhone if you lose your phone. You must have Apple ID before you can perform this function.

Let's get started.

- Tap on **Settings** on the Home screen of your device.

- Tap on your **Apple ID** which appears as your name at the top of settings page.

- Scroll down and tap on **iCloud.**

- Toggle the indicator next to '**iCloud Drive'** to turn the feature On. With this feature turned On, you can sync all your documents with other devices using **iCloud.**

- Tap on **Photos** on the iCloud page.

- Scroll down and turn On **'Upload to My Photos Stream**.' This feature when turned On automatically syncs all new pictures on your device with other devices on your iCloud.

- Return to the **iCloud** page.

- Turn On the indicators on all the data files you want to sync.

- Tap on the home button to return to the home screen.

How to set up and Use screen time

Screen time allows you to get an overview of how much time you use your iPhone. With screen time you can set time limits on some apps especially the apps you are addicted to. This will help you manage the time you spend on your device.

To set up and use screen time:

- Tap on **Settings** on the Home screen of your device.

- Scroll to the bottom of settings page and tap on **Screen Time.**

- Tap on **See All Activity** on screen time page.

- The use of your device the previous week is displayed next to total screen time.

- Select **Day** at the top of the screen.

- That particular day's use will be displayed at the top.

- Return to **Screen Time** page.

- Scroll down and tap on **Share Across Devices.** Turn the function On and follow the on-screen instructions to turn total screen across all of your devices On/Off. With this feature turned On, you can see Screen Time for all your devices.

- On the next page, tap on **Ignore Limit.** This will notify you if you have used your assigned screen time.

- On the next page, select the required settings.

- To turn off screen time, return to Screen Time Page and scroll down to the end of the page and tap **Turn Off Screen Time.**

- Confirm your request when prompted.

- Tap on the home button to return to the home screen.

How to set up Find My iPhone Feature.

The find my iPhone feature helps you find your iPhone when you lose it, or you can lock it when it is stolen. To enable this feature, you need to have an Apple ID.

To set up Find My iPhone:

- Tap on **Settings** on the Home screen of your device.

- Tap on your **Apple ID.**

- Scroll down and tap on **Find My.**

- Tap on **Find My iPhone.**

- Turn it On by toggling the indicator next to it.

- Turn On **Enable Offline Finding.** When you turn On this function, follow the on-screen instructions to finish activation. When this feature is activated, your iPhone can use other nearby Apple devices to register its current location through Bluetooth.

- Scroll down and turn on **Send Last Location.** With this function turned on, your iPhone can send its current location regularly to iCloud using GPS or Wi-Fi networks.

- Tap on the home button to return to the home screen.

How to Find your iPhone when lost or stolen.
The Find My iPhone feature enables you to find

your mobile device if you lose it or it gets stolen.

You can also lock it.

To find your iPhone:

- Open a browser on your computer and go to

  www.icloud.com.

- Click on **Find My iPhone.**

- Click on **All Devices** at the top of the screen.

- A list of devices will be displayed, click on
  the name of your mobile device.

- The latest position of your iPhone device
  will be displayed on the Map.

- Click on **Play Sound**. If your device is connected is on and connected to a mobile network or Wi-Fi, it will play a sound for two minutes.

- Click **Lost Mode** and follow the on-screen instructions to lock your iPhone. You can lock your iPhone with a code and also add a message on the screen saying that you have lost your iPhone. If your Offline Finding is

On, you can see the latest position of your iPhone.

- Click on **'Erase iPhone'** and follow the on-screen instructions to wipe all your phone content. If you delete all phone content, you will no longer be able to use Find My iPhone.

Chapter Six

Camera.

How to take pictures with your phone.

- Tap on the **Camera App** on the home

  screen of your device.

- Tap on **PHOTO** on the screen of your

  device to put your device on picture mode.

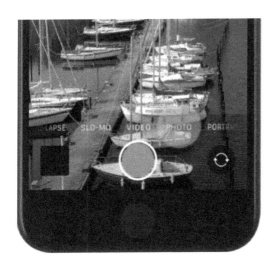

- Tap on the **Flash Icon** at the top left corner of your device screen.

- Point the camera lens at the back of your device to the required object.

- On the screen of your device, drag two fingers together or apart to zoom in or out.

- Tap on the take picture icon to take a photo.

- Tap on the home button to return to the home screen.

How to record a video.
You can record a video with your iPhone device.

To record a video:

- Tap on the **Camera App** on the home screen of your device.

- Tap on **VIDEO** on the screen of your device.

- Tap on the video light icon at the top left corner of your device screen.

- Point the camera lens at the back of your device to the required object.

- On the screen of your device, drag two fingers together or apart to zoom in or out.

- Tap on the record icon to start recording a video.

- Tap the stop icon to stop recording a video.

- Tap on the home button to return to the home screen.

How to view pictures and video clips.
You can view pictures you took and video you

made on your device gallery.

To view pictures and video clips:

- Tap on Photos App on the home screen of

  your device.

- Go to the required folder and tap on the picture or video.

- Tap on the home button to return to the home screen.

How to send a picture or video clip in an MMS.

You can send a picture or a video clip as a multi-Media message. Take the following steps to get started.

- Tap on the **Photos app** on the home screen of your device.

- Tap on the picture or video clip you wish to send.

- Tap on the share icon.

- Tap on **messages.**

- Tap on To and enter the recipients contact.

- Tap on the text input fiend and enter your message then tap **SEND.**

- The green arrow up icon is the send icon.

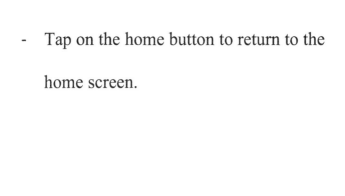

- Tap on the home button to return to the home screen.

How to send pictures or videos via email.

You can send a picture or video in an email.

To send a picture or video through email:

- Tap on the **Photos app** on the home screen of your device.

- Tap on the picture or video clip you wish to send.

- Tap on the **share icon.**

- Tap on the **Mail icon.**

- Tap on To and enter the recipients email
  address.

- Tap on **Subject** and enter the subject of the
  email.

- Type an accompanying email on the body of
  the mail.

- Tap on the send icon.

- Tap on the home button to return to the
  home screen.

How to take a screenshot.
You can take a picture of your screen if you want

to share whatever you are viewing or reading with

a friend. You take a screenshot and send it to them.

To take a screenshot:

- Tap on the Power button and the home

  button together to take a screenshot.

- Tap on the screenshot immediately after it

  got captured to edit it.

- To send it to a friend, go through the Photos app.

Chapter Seven

Global Services.

How to install Facebook on your iPhone device.
To use Facebook on your device, you need to have it installed. To install Facebook, you need to set up your device for internet ad have your Apple ID.

To install Facebook:

- Tap on the App Store app on the home screen of your device.

- On the app store page, tap on the search icon at the bottom right side of your device.

- Type Facebook on the search bar and click on the first option.

- On Facebook page, tap on GET and follow the instructions on the screen of your device to get it installed.

- Tap on the home button to return to the home screen.

Follow the above steps to install every other relevant Apps you want.